POSITIONED TO LIVE

Tammy Graves

TABLE OF CONTENTS

ABOUT THE AUTHOR

Tammy Graves is the founder and Pastor of Oasis Outreach Ministries and is also an Occupational Safety Specialist with Tennessee OSHA. She holds a Master of Business Administration degree from Union University, a Bachelor of Science degree from Middle Tennessee State University and an Associate of Science degree in Pre-Med from Jackson State Community College. Ms. Graves attended Memphis Bible Institute and served her country for six years in the United States Army Reserves. She has been a guest speaker at numerous seminars, conferences, and summits. She enjoys freelance writing, reading, public speaking, teaching, running, cooking and traveling. She's also a certified personal trainer. Ms. Graves is a resident of Jackson, Tennessee.

ACKNOWLEDGEMENTS

This book was conceived in 2007. The Lord kept saying wait; it is not time. He began to impart more revelation and insight over the years. This year He said, "Now is the appointed time"; nine years later. I thank God for His timing and for knowing what His people need and when they need it. I dedicate this book to the most important person in my life – Jesus. Lord Jesus, you are the love of my soul. Thank you for choosing me and for my position in your Kingdom. I hope that I have pleased you.

I thank my spiritual father and mentor, Bishop Elroy Hicks, for seeing who I am when I could not. I thank you for your patience, compassion and love. Thank you for being to me and for me what others forfeited. I love you Bishop.

I thank Prophetess Margaret White, for being my Samuel and my Nathan when the wilderness seemed endless. Your love has been unconditional and has strengthened me through my make over. I love you Mother.

I thank Dorinda Myles, for being unselfish and pouring into me in the time of famine. Your trust and friendship has been a breath of fresh air. I love you my true friend.

INTRODUCTION

"You weren't born just to live a life and to die; you were born to accomplish something specifically."— Dr. Myles Munroe

The Spirit of the Lord is upon me,
Because he hath anointed me
To preach the gospel to the poor;
He hath sent me to heal the brokenhearted,
To preach deliverance to the captives
And recovering of sight to the blind,
To set at liberty them that are bruised;
To preach the acceptable year of the Lord.
— Luke 4:18-19

Today the Spirit of the Lord is grieved because we have not allowed Him to come upon us but rather, the spirit of lack and the spirit of emotionalism have become the center- piece of the follower of Jesus Christ's spiritual table. Therefore, the follower of Jesus Christ is being deprived of the spiritual nutrients the Holy Spirit desires to feed because of the traditional meals of religion served during supper. This contributes to the disjointed Church operating outside of its commission and to its spiritual disorientation.

The Church has allowed the world to influence and dictate its worship and its relationship with God. In order for the Church to engage in the apostolic and prophetic worship, it must begin to operate under the apostolic and prophetic anointing. It must tear down all the generational idols and superficial foundations of men. The five-fold ministry must become fitly and joined together. In the book of Ephesians, Apostle Paul tells the Church that one of the results of being redeemed in Jesus Christ is being united in one household, one body, one Church, with the habitation of God.

"Now therefore ye are no more strangers and foreigners, but fellow-citizens with the saints, and of the household of God; And are built upon the foundation of the apostles and prophets, Jesus Christ himself being the chief corner stone; In whom all the building fitly framed together growth unto an holy temple in the Lord: In whom ye also are built together for an habitation of God through the Spirit." — Ephesians 2:19-22

Although there is one body, one Spirit, one hope of our calling, each follower of Jesus Christ must take up his called and chosen position and begin to walk out his assignment.
"And he gave some, apostles; and some, prophets; and some, evangelists; and some, pastors and teachers; For the perfecting of

the saints, for the work of the ministry, for the edifying of the body of Christ: Till we all come in the unity of faith, and of the knowledge of the Son of God, unto a perfect man, unto the measure of the stature of the fullness of Christ: That we henceforth be no more children, tossed to and fro, and carried about with every wind of doctrine, by the sleight of men, and cunning craftiness, whereby they lie in wait to deceive; But speaking truth in love, may grow up into him in all things, which is the head, even Christ: From whom the whole body fitly joined together compacted by that which every joint supplieth, according to the effectual working in the measure of every part, maketh increase of the body unto the edifying of itself in love."
— Ephesians 4:11-16

When we, the followers of Jesus Christ, go from hearing the word, to understanding the revelation of the word, to application, we will then be carriers of the presence of God by day and by night. We will be Glory Carriers. We will walk together in our respective positions carrying out our mandated assignments in the Spirit of unity; God's total agreement plan. As a result, we will see the poor prosper; the brokenhearted mended; the captives freed; the blind having sight; the bruised liberated and the acceptable year of the Lord manifested daily. Saints will no longer struggle with the same tests and trials because their faith will have become perfected and the knowledge of Jesus Christ will have been formed in them through relationship — His presence — will have perfected their anointing and the love of God within them.

As sons of God, each is required to obey the totality of God's word so that he may receive His presence, keep His presence, and obtain the blessings from the Father's presence. I am convinced, by the enlightenment of the eyes of my understanding through the Holy Spirit, that God is now ushering us to understand the correlation of His presence and the Ark of the Covenant. There are specific things that one must do to partake of the presence of God and to have His presence remain with them. I believe God has given me revelation and anointed this book to empower you with the wisdom and knowledge of God's presence. God desires to give you a vast understanding of the importance of carrying out your assignment. As you begin to read, open your heart and you shall receive specific instructions from God concerning your purpose on this earth. We have dominion and we have the instructions to penetrate, subdue, overtake and recover all.

CHAPTER ONE
POSITIONED FOR THE PRESENCE

Jesus' positions and titles are forever infinite and eternal. No man can nor will ever have as many positions in the Kingdom of God as Jesus. Jesus' assignment while on the earth was to do the will of God; to lay down his life to pay the debt for our sins and to destroy the works of Satan. Jesus' positions are manifested as an Apostle, Prophet, Evangelist, Pastor, Teacher, the Way, the Truth, the Life, the true Vine, the Healer, the Deliverer, the Lord of Lords, the King of Kings, the Prince of Peace, the Bright Morning Star, the Lily of the Valley, Alpha, Omega, the Beginning, the End, Savior, Advocate, Holy One, the Chief Cornerstone, Good Shepherd, Anointed One, Beloved Son, Bread of Life, Bridegroom, Root of David, Master, Rabbi, Author, Finisher and many others.

We have been placed on the earth with a Kingdom position and a Kingdom assignment. There is a set time in which the Holy Spirit descends upon us to manifest the revealing of the position. Jesus' mother, Mary wanted Jesus to reveal his position before time. At the wedding reception in Cana, Jesus says to Mary, "My hour has not yet come" (John 2:4). And when it was time for the revealing of his position, the presence appeared. The Holy Spirit descended upon him in a form like a dove and all power and authority in heaven and on earth He was.

What happens when the chosen dies? What happened when Moses, Aaron, Joshua and Samson died? What happens when the apostolic and the prophetic anointing dies? What happens when the judges die; when the high priest allows sin to enter into the tabernacle? The presence of God leaves; until God anoints and appoints someone in the position with the assignment of positioning the people to live in His presence. Notice the key word − live. How do you live in the presence? How do you make the presence your permanent residence? You must be positioned to live in the presence of God. What does this mean? It means you must be in the position God has assigned you and performing the assignment God has assigned you. This is the only way you can handle the weight of His presence. This is the only way you can be a Glory Carrier. The presence is tangible. It is the secret place of the Most High God. Those who dwell in this place are living in this place from sun up to sun down. No matter where they go or who comes into their presence; life happens. The presence comes to give us the more abundant life; to live the purpose. Let's go to the scriptures and take a look at the sequence of events which led to a man dying while carrying the presence of God. Let us look at 1 Chronicles 13 and 1 Samuel 3:

> ➢ The ark represents the presence of God and the children of Israel had traveled with it for years
> ➢ The children of Israel began to turn their backs on God and worship idols and let sin come into their hearts
> ➢ Moses, Aaron, Joshua and Samson died
> ➢ There is no presence of the Apostolic and Prophetic anointing
> ➢ The judges are dead
> ➢ The presence of God (The Ark of the Covenant) was in the Temple
> ➢ Eli was the high priest in charge of the Tabernacle

16

- Eli watched over the Ark of the Covenant
- Eli allowed sin to encamp in the House of God
- Eli allowed his sons to commit sin and they had no reverence for God in the Tabernacle
- God calls Samuel to the prophetic ministry and Samuel prophesies judgment on Eli and his sons
- The children of Israel go to war with the Philistines and realize they need God's presence
- The children of Israel carry the Ark of the Covenant to the battlefield
- 30,000 soldiers are killed
- The Philistines defeat them and take the Ark of the Covenant
- The Philistines take the Ark of the Covenant to Ashdod
- The Philistines place it in their temple beside their idol god Dagon
- The next day they discover Dagon had fallen over
- The day after, they discover Dagon had fallen over again; this time with his hands and head cut off
- Plagues and tumors break out
- The Philistines take the Ark of the Covenant to Gath, Ekron
- The people cry send it back to its people with a trespass offering
- They send it on a new cart with two fresh cows pulling it
- The Ark of the Covenant goes to Beth-Shemesh
- The people rejoice and look inside; God kills 70 men for looking inside
- The Ark of the Covenant is sent to Kirth-jearim to Abinadab's house and it stays 20 years
- Saul becomes king
- Saul is rejected by God
- David is anointed by God
- David defeats Goliath

- ➤ Saul tries to kill David
- ➤ David spares Saul's life twice
- ➤ Saul dies
- ➤ David's set time as king manifests; revealing his position

We will examine David's role in the death of a man; while obeying his king's orders, in chapter three.

CHAPTER TWO
IN HIS PRESENCE

According to the word of God there are prerequisites, conditions, and a lifestyle that the Body of Christ must choose in order to receive, to walk in, and to remain in God's presence. First, the Body of Christ must obey God's instructions — His word. There are many chosen men and women in the bible that obeyed God. One of them was Moses; a prophet, whom God himself called His friend. Through obedience, Moses experienced the presence of God daily from sun up to sun down. "For the cloud of the Lord was above the tabernacle by day and fire was over it by night" (Exodus 40:38).

Second, the Body of Christ must give God an offering willingly with its heart. "Then the Lord spoke to Moses saying: speak to the children of Israel, that they bring Me an offering. From everyone that gives it willingly with his heart, you shall take from them: gold, silver, and bronze; blue purple and scarlet thread, fine linen, and goats hair, rams skins dyed red, badger's skins, and acacia wood; oil for the light and spices for the anointing oil and for the sweet incense; onyx stones and stones to be set in the ephod and in the breastplate. And let them make Me a sanctuary, that I may dwell among them" (Exodus 25:1-8).

As followers of Jesus Christ, we must be willing to totally surrender our will and our desires for the will and desires of God. We must offer Him from our hearts that which is of value —

relationship; quality time. We like Jesus, must lay down our life in order to receive the presence of God among us. When His presence comes, He shows us all things that He himself does and He assigns to us greater works. He empowers us to do the greater works and; we will accomplish them if we allow Him to dwell among us.

Third, each of us in the Body of Christ must remain in the position God has appointed unto us until the appointed time expires. The expired time will either come as a reassignment or physical death. At times, God will restructure the plan or He will allow the vision to pass on to the Joshua and the Elijah he raises up beside you. Having been in the Army Reserves for six years, and having worked in corporate America for many years, I have experienced the pyramid of rank and position.

I know that each rank and/or position is under the authority of another. And there are consequences for breaking rank and yielding your flesh to insubordination. One is a demotion in position and in rank. Another is a dishonorable discharge from service. The kingdom of God encompasses the same principle.

Whenever a soldier breaks rank and gets out of position, he or she puts the rest of the soldiers in danger. Too many saints have left their position, assigned by God, in the kingdom of God and began to operate in another. Therefore, they have trespassed against the will of God and brought a curse of spiritual death upon the Body of Christ and the ministry they are positioned in. As a result, the presence of God is not moving to and fro in our midst because of our disobedience.

Each follower of Jesus Christ has an ordained position and an ordained assignment in the Body of Christ. God has spoken them into existence and He has labeled them "the most holy things".

The entire fourth chapter of Numbers deals with positions and assignments. God tells Moses and Aaron not to cut off the tribe of the families of the Kohathites from the Levites, but instead appoint each of them to his service and his task. God said after they had been given their assignment, if they watched while the most holy things were being covered (this was the assignment given to Aaron and his sons), they would die.

Their assignment was to carry the most holy things, not to cover them. In order for our ministries to give birth, they must remain fertile. They must not ever take on the assignment of another ministry, lest they will surely die. We must prepare our spirit to follow God's directions while traveling on our assigned path. When we place ourselves in someone else's position and we do what God has appointed them to do, we not only die at the threshing floor, putting aside His presence, but we allow a false anointing to reside. For this reason alone, many ministries never advance to the next level. God is eternal and His anointing is eternal. Therefore, if He has anointed us and has placed us in the position He willed before the foundation of the earth, then our position is a spiritual blessing and it is a heavenly place in Christ.

God is eternal and His anointing is eternal. Our positions are of His good pleasure and we (the Body of Christ) are positioned to know the hope of His calling; to have a relationship.

Paul expounds upon this to the Ephesian believers in Ephesians 1:1-23. Paul says, that "the God of our Lord Jesus Christ, the Father of glory, may give unto you the spirit of wisdom and revelation in the knowledge of him: The eyes of your understanding being enlightened; that ye may know what is the hope of his calling, and what the riches of the glory of his inheritance in the saints, And what is the exceeding greatness of his power to us-ward who believe, according to the working of his mighty power, which he wrought in Christ, when he raised him from the dead, and set him at his own right hand in the heavenly places, far above all principality, and power and might, and dominion, and every name that is named, not only in this world, but also in that which is to come: And hath put all things under his feet, and gave him to be the head over all things to the church, which is his body, the fullness of him that filleth all in all" (Ephesians 1:17-23). The Body of Christ consists of different positions with different assignments but all positions have a common denominator — Jesus Christ, the chief cornerstone, who is positioned at the right hand of God.

Next, the Body of Christ must rid itself of everything that is unclean and impure. This includes people in your circle who are not willing to receive their deliverance and wholeness. Moses was commissioned by God to command the children of Israel to put every leper, everyone that had an issue, and whosoever was defiled by the dead, out of the camp (Numbers 5:1-5). In order for the presence of God to manifest and dwell in our life, we must repent of our sins and be washed in the blood of Jesus. There must not be anything in our life that will separate us from the presence of God. In Romans 8:35-39, Paul asks the question: "Who shall separate us from the love of Christ?" The answer is nothing separates us from Christ's love however, sin and an unclean, impure life separates you from His presence.

One night in the spring of 1999, the Lord visited me; while I was asleep. He took my spirit out of my body and we went to Hell. I could not see Him; I could only feel His presence and His love. While there, he allowed me to experience different physical aspects. First, I felt His presence. Then I felt my flesh burning. It began to peel; without being consumed. I smelt the stench of burning flesh. Next, there was memory of each opportunity that was given to receive Him and His presence. It was played over and over in your mind like a movie. Then I felt loneliness. He had left me. His presence was gone. A feeling of indescribable fear overwhelmed me and as quickly as His presence had left, Jesus positioned himself there with me again. He then spoke these words, "Tell my people Hell is real." At that moment I realized although God is omnipresent, His presence does not and will not reside in Hell. Immediately, my spirit was back in my body.

CHAPTER THREE
RIGHT POSITION WRONG ASSIGNMENT

II Samuel 6:1-6 and I Chronicles 13:1-9 give the account of the Ark of the Covenant, which represents the presence of God, being brought back to Jerusalem by King David. David gathered 30,000 troops and went to Baal Judah also called Kirjath-jearim, to Abinadab's house to obtain the Ark of the Covenant. Abinadab had two sons Uzza and Ahio, which were placed in charge of moving the Ark of the Covenant. Uzza and Ahio placed the Ark of the Covenant on a new cart and carried it out of their father's house. Ahio walked out front with the oxen, as Uzza rode on the cart with the Ark of the Covenant.

David and all of Israel were rejoicing, singing, praising, and magnifying God for His presence being with them once again. David and his men reached Nachon and there was a dip in the road. As the oxen crossed the dip, they stumbled and the cart began to slide. Uzza, riding on the cart with the Ark of the Covenant, reached his hand back and grabbed the Ark of the Covenant to keep it from falling. By touching the Ark of the Covenant, Uzza made God angry. God smote Uzza and he fell dead beside the Ark of the Covenant.

Why would God kill a man for touching the Ark of the Covenant? In Exodus 25:10-16, God tells Moses to tell the children of Israel to make him an ark of Acacia wood three and three quarters feet long, two and one quarter feet wide and two and one quarter feet high. They were instructed to overlay the inside and outside with pure gold and a molding of gold all around it. Then they were instructed to cast four gold rings and attach them to the four corners of the ark; two on each side. Two poles were inserted into the rings so that the Ark could be carried. God said the poles should remain in the rings of the Ark permanently so that the Ark could not be touched. They were not supposed to be removed from the Ark.

God told Moses to tell his chosen people to build the Ark and what material they were to use to build it. God even told Moses who was assigned to touch it and who was assigned to carry it (using the golden Acacia poles). In Numbers 4:1-6, God tells Moses and Aaron to take a census and count the number of Kohath family members in the Levi tribe. God tells them to count all males from the age of 30-50 who were able to work in the Tabernacle. God assigns each his specific sacred duty. When the camp moved, Aaron and his sons were assigned to go in the Tabernacle first.

They were assigned to take down the veil and to cover the Ark of the Covenant with it. After covering the Ark of the Covenant with the veil, they were assigned to cover the veil with goatskin leather and to cover the goatskin leather with blue cloth and place the carrying poles in the rings. Next, they were assigned to cover the other holy things: the lamp stand, the table of showbread, the dishes, the instruments and the altar. After Aaron and his sons finished their assignment, the men from the Kohath family from the age of 30-50 who were able to work in the Tabernacle, who were assigned to go in and to carry the most holy things to wherever the camp was traveling.

God commanded the Kohathites not to touch the most holy things uncovered lest they die. So, the Kohathites had not only been given a position as servants in the Tabernacle (the Church) but they had also been given their assignment in the Tabernacle (the Church). Moses and Aaron were positioned by God as leaders. They were given the assignment to make sure each man knew his assignment and to make sure each man was positioned to live; while serving and performing his sacred duty in his appointed assignment.

Oftentimes, we go to the House of God and we praise, we magnify the name of Jesus, we dance, we shout, we speak in other tongues and we bless the Lord. We feel as if we have obeyed God's word and that we have done the right thing all week long. But when we get to the threshing floor, when we get to Nachon, when trials and tests and tribulation and persecution come and our faith begins to slip and slide and we reach for the Ark (His presence), asking the question, "Lord where are you?", we experience a spiritual death.

Today, the Church is experiencing the spiritual death of Uzza — a separation from the presence of God. The called and the chosen have taken on the wrong assignment. We have been given God's specific instructions, but we have handled the most holy things in an improper manner. Uzza was in the right position to carry the Ark of the Covenant. He was of the Kohathite blood line; however, he took upon himself the wrong assignment by touching it. He was not to touch the Ark of the Covenant because he was not the High Priest or the son of the High Priest. God had not given Uzza the assignment of Aaron's son Eleazar, which was the supervision of everything in the Tabernacle. Many followers of Jesus Christ have taken on assignments, which they think fit their position, but have not been approved by God. The usher is trying to be the deacon, the deacon is trying to be the choir director, the choir director is trying to be the treasurer, the treasurer is trying to be the armor bearer, the armor bearer is trying to be the musician, and the musician is trying to be the pastor.

The presence of God cannot come in the Tabernacle and dwell among us because God's due order, God's positioning and God's assignments are not being downloaded with precision by the overseer/shepherd in order to effectively communicate it to the people of God. Unlike Moses and Aaron, today many leaders are not following divine instructions from God pertaining to positioning and assignments. They have not set up proper order in their ministries, but rather engage in the political aspect of positioning. Instead of listening to and obeying the commands of God concerning filling each office, each duty, each position and each assignment, leaders make their decisions based on fleshly desires of: pleasing friends and family, longevity of their members and catering to the substantial tithers. Thus, they cause Uzza (the follower of Jesus Christ) to die while serving in ministry.

God told Moses and Aaron, who were positioned by God as leaders, that their assignment was inclusive; to not let the Kohath family destroy themselves. God gave them specific instructions. God said Moses and Aaron must make sure that Aaron and his sons go in with the Kohath men and point out what each is to carry so that they would not die when they carried the "most holy" things. Otherwise, they could never enter the sanctuary for even a moment. For, if they were alone and looked upon the sacred objects, they would die. Many in the Tabernacle (Church) are not being properly mentored. They are not being instructed on the consequences of performing assignments/duties that have not been validated by God through the "most holy" thing on Earth — the Holy Spirit.

David allowed Uzza and Ahio to disobey God's instructions on how to carry the Ark of the Covenant. Instead of placing the poles through the golden rings, they placed it on a new cart and allowed a mule to pull it. This act of disobedience is what the Tabernacle (Church) has gotten accustom to. We want the title, we want the position but, we do not want to carry the burden that comes with the position's assignment. We would rather ride on the cart and be seen, while others carry out the assignment and reap the consequences of being out of position.

"To obey is better than sacrifice" (I Samuel 15: 22). Obeying and hearkening to God's word is exceedingly more rewarding than dying in the fullness of your ministry. Disobedience is rebellion and "rebellion is as the sin of witchcraft" (I Samuel 15:23), fettering the presence of God. As a result, yokes are not being destroyed off of the necks of the children of God. The supernatural manifestation of deliverance is stagnated at the threshing floor because the "most holy" thing (the presence of God) has not been handled properly. Therefore, we can not be the effective witnesses of Acts 1:8, "but ye shall receive power, after that the Holy Ghost is come upon you: and ye shall be witnesses unto me both in Jerusalem, and in all Judaea, and in Samaria, and unto the uttermost part of the earth."

The apostle, the prophet, the evangelist, the pastor, and the teacher then finds himself/herself in the position of David, along with the people of God at Perezuzza and wondering, How shall Ark of the Lord come to me? How shall the presence of God come to me? How shall the Ark of the Lord come to our city? How shall the presence of God come to our house?

30

CHAPTER FOUR
DON'T ACCEPT THE POSITION: BE THE POSITION

True Apostles and true Pastors are representatives of God's Ark. They carry the manna, which represents the word of God. They are positioned in the Kingdom of God to feed the sheep because of their love for Jesus; with knowledge and understanding. They carry Aaron's rod, which represents the power and authority of God. And they carry the commandments of God, which represent a lifestyle of total submission to God and full obedience. They lead God's sheep through the wilderness, through Jordan, through the land of Canaan, through Jericho to Jerusalem. This generation of leaders must possess keen insight in the Spirit. They must not get caught up into the title of apostle, prophet, evangelist, pastor or teacher. They must do the work of the service, and that is bearing the burdens in the tabernacle. They must not just accept the position; they must be the position. They must be the priests who intercede for the people in the land while under the authority of El Roi, the God who sees. They must not worship idol gods, which includes themselves.

Instead, they have to be willing to receive step-by-step instructions from the Throne of Heaven. Upon receiving their instructions, they must not be afraid to carry out Heaven's orders. The word of God tells us that many are called but few are chosen. Today's leaders have become legalistic and political minded and have dawned on the ideology of what society deems as a true man or woman of God. They have begun to care more for themselves and their image and their ego; than for their flock. This misrepresentation of the love, the character and the heart of God will be judged. The book of Ezekiel attests to Israel's shepherds being judged. They were removed from their position and held accountable for the sheep they were supposed to lead. God, positioned as our All Mighty God, is going to gather the sheep and rescue them from the places where they have been scattered.

These places represent the disposition of the Body of Christ in ministries, in callings, in careers, in cities, in states, and in countries. God is going to reposition them back into their destined position and strengthen those that have grown weak. Picture a dislocated joint that has to be set and repositioned back into its proper place. This explains why there is so much pain and discomfort in the Body of Christ; it has been dislocated and disposition beyond its time and its season. Therefore, God is supernaturally resetting the dislocation of the Body of Christ so that, in these last days, it will be again fitly and joined together supplying edification to all members as well as reaping in the harvest. After the flock has been brought back into its proper predestined position, God is going to shower down His presence upon them like never before. They shall be free from the yoke of bondage and live in the presence of God and they shall be secure in the anointing. Once a dislocated joint is repositioned, it begins to receive the proper blood flow. The proper blood flow catalyses the healing process of any bruised or pulled ligaments, tendons and muscles.

Proper positioning is the catalyst for the anointing of God to flow and bring about expedient, exceedingly, abundant manifestations of the authority and power of God. The accelerated glory of God will then manifest signs, miracles and wonders; it will advance deliverance and healing ministries.

The position is not only an assignment, it is an inheritance. An inheritance is defined as the practice of passing on property, titles, debt, rights, and obligations upon the death of a person. The one who leaves the inheritance is called the predecessor. The predecessor is the person who held the office or position. The one who is "legally" entitled to the property and rank of another on the person's death is called the heir/successor. Notice I stated, on the person's death and not after. Being legally entitled to the property and rank of another on the person's death, means before that person dies. Therefore, the heir has already been selected, manifested (revealed), and inaugurated before God and before the people. The heir not only represents a passing on of property, titles, debt, rights and obligations; it is also a continuation of the predecessor's legacy. If there is a spirit of control ruling the predecessor, there will never be a practice of passing on. The Apostle and the Prophet can inaugurate the inheritance, which is a representation of anointing, conferring, appointing and declaring. After the position has been conferred on the heir, it is the heir's obligation to accept the pass on and convert it to a pass over. A pass over is the manifested work(s) of the pass on or the increase of the fruit of the work(s) revealed.

We should not only accept our positions in Jesus, we should be His heir in the Spirit. Who was given Elijah's mantle? Who had a double portion of Elijah's anointing conferred on them? Elisha accepted the mantle and the anointing. Elisha was the mantle and the anointing. Elijah did not practice a spirit of controlling the passing on, instead he conferred assignments upon Hazael, Jehu and Elisha which we will discussed in chapter six.

CHAPTER FIVE
PROPER ALIGNMENT FOR THE GREATER WORKS

I believe we are entering a season of proper alignment. The Church is about to shift into a proper alignment of spiritual offices and an Elijah anointing that Elisha himself never imagined to see. As this alignment and positioning transpire, ministry will then shift to the other side. Saints will begin to flow in the abundance of the anointing and we will see miracles, signs and wonders, being wrought as never before seen. In Matthew Chapter 14, Jesus hears of John the Baptist's murder (beheading) from John's disciples. Jesus gets into a boat and rows away to a deserted place to be alone.

A multitude of people from many villages see where He is headed and follow Him by foot. When Jesus comes out of the wilderness, out of the deserted place, the large crowd awaits Him. Jesus is moved with compassion and begins to minister to them. He begins to heal them. He ministers over into the evening and as night approaches, the disciples bring to His attention that they are in a deserted place and that it is past dinner. The disciples admonish Jesus to send the people home to their villages so that they can buy themselves something to eat. Jesus turns to His disciples and says that will not be necessary, "you feed them". The word of God says, "Blessed are they, which hunger and thirst after righteousness: for they shall be filled", (Matthew 5:6). Jesus had feed them spiritually and now He had to meet a natural need. The disciples were shocked and in disbelief that he would even suggest a silly thing. They replied, "We only have five loaves of bread and two fish." Jesus says, "Bring it to Me." Jesus tells the people to sit down on the grass and He takes the fish and bread and offers it up to the Father and asks Him to bless the meal and He begins to break the loaves. He passes the broken pieces of bread to the disciples to pass out. Five thousand men, not including the women and children, ate until they were full. Twelve baskets were left over.

The lame will walk, the deaf will hear, the mute will speak. Deliverance will arise to the greater works level in this shift; this proper alignment. The Body of Christ is going to experience such a manifestation because the Holy Spirit is going to reassign and rearrange man's agendas. In this shift, leaders are going to completely humble to the will and workings of the Holy Spirit, as it redirects their steps and repositions them in ministries and most importantly in the kingdom of God. Jesus tells the disciples to take their boat and go ahead of Him to the other side. He would meet them there. As the disciples get into the boat, Jesus gets the people to begin to return home and He goes up into the mountains to be alone. Meanwhile, the disciples are out on the sea and in trouble. The wind and waves toss the ship to and fro. The disciples grow scared. Around four a.m., in the midst of the storm, they see an image and they are frightened; believing it is a ghost. It is Jesus walking on the water and He calls out to them, "be of good cheer it is I, don't be afraid." Peter says, "Lord if it is you bid me to come." And Jesus says, "Come." Peter steps out of the boat and begins to walk on the water until he loses focus and no longer sees Jesus. Instead, he sees his environment and the atmosphere. Peter begins to sink and he cries out, "Lord, save me!"

Today, this cry is echoing in the hearts of many followers of Jesus Christ. They have seen miracles happen in their lives and in the lives of others; just as the disciples had seen. However, seeing thousands of people fed and healed does not prepare us for ministry on the other side. The multitude being fed did not produce exceedingly abundant faith in any of the disciples. Even the word that Jesus taught the people did not position them in their faith. Yes, faith cometh by hearing and hearing by the word of God. However, like us the disciples had spent ample time alone with Jesus — who had imparted the word into them and had spoken the mysteries of God to them. Yet, they went on their way to the other side unprepared. They went misaligned. They went in the wrong position. They went as followers; disciples and not as apostles; sent ones. The beloved John said, "For this reason was the son of man manifested, that He might destroy the works of the devil." For this reason you and I have been sent to cast out demons because we have been positioned in His power against unclean spirits.

We have been sent to heal all manner of sickness and all manner of disease. The cry on the inside of you is the same groan and travail of creation, crying out for the alignment of the Body of Christ; of the sons of God. Your spirit knows that on the other side lies another level of healing and deliverance. On the other side is the Elijah anointing. On the other side is transfiguration. On the other side is revelation knowledge. On the other side are higher ranking principalities, higher ranking powers, higher ranking rulers of darkness of this world and higher ranking spiritual wickedness in high places. On the other side is the supernatural ability and accelerated glory to tread on serpents and scorpions, and over all the power of the enemy. Nothing harms us or stops the greater works on the other side. On the other side, we run through troops and leap over walls.

Your cry is because your King David has not positioned you to live, as your King Jesus says "go to the other side." When you cross over to the other side, you must already be in your assigned position. The position is not assigned by King David, which represents your leader. The position is assigned by the King of Kings–God. The other side not only contains a land flowing with milk and honey; it contains the ripened harvest.

In Uzza's days, there was not any machinery. So after the harvest, the grain was separated manually from the straw and the husk; by beating it. The threshing floor was a flat, hard and smooth surface. The sheaves were spread on the threshing floor and oxen and cattle tread over them repeatedly to loosen and separate the edible grain from the inedible grain. The threshing floor is the place on the other side where your position and assignment is tread upon repeatedly to separate the position assigned by God and the position given by man.

CHAPTER SIX
SPIRITUAL LOCATION

There is a question that I want you to ponder on as you continue to read this book. The question is a relatively simple question; yet revelatory. Each word is powerful but it cannot stand alone. Each word must come together so that the reader, which is you, will be able to respond. Your response is vital to your future and to the next phase of your life. I recommend that you allow the words of the question to penetrate and saturate your inner spirit before answering. I even suggest that you wait until you have read the last word of this book to answer this: "Will You Tarry in Gilgal or Will You Relocate?"

God is doing a new thing; this new thing is a set time for a set-up. God is trying to renovate your mind, renew your mind and reconstruct your mind. He is trying to take your ways of thinking, your habitual thoughts, and your thought patterns which have been passed down from generation to generation to you, and replace them with the thoughts and thinking of Jesus Christ.

God wants you to allow Him to break the cycle of the system's mindsets that are built up in you. What are these systems? Your customs, traditions, heritage, education, government, religion, economy and even family are representatives of a system. You have throughout your existence on this earth gleamed from each to think the way you think. God has to start construction on your mind first before he moves you to another place in Him spiritually. He has to renew your mind as a part of the process of your spiritual growth.

We enter this world as an infant however; we do not remain in the infant stage of life. We begin to grow and to mature. Regardless of an infant's shape, size, race, or demographic location, every infant is going to grow and develop when it is placed in an environment that is conducive for growth. This is the case also for spiritual growth. God's spiritual growth plan he has designed for your life is not for you to remain in the same place for the rest of your life. It is a progressive plan. Infant, Toddler, Pre-Schooler, School Aged Child, Adolescent, Young Adult, Middle Aged Adult, and Older Adult are the stages of our natural and physical growth and development. Hence, there is a spiritual growth and development stage in which you have to relocate to. You cannot stay in the same spiritual place.

Naturally, most have not stayed in the same physical location. Meaning, most people are not living in the same house they grew up in. They grew up; they matured and they left. They moved; they relocated. As an infant up until I became a teenager I lived on Brooks Lane. At the age of fourteen, we moved to Ed Wood Road. When I became a young adult I moved to another state and I have made several moves since that time. Growth and development requires action. It requires a change. It requires a move; a relocation. Isaiah 43:18-20 says, "Remember ye not the former things, neither consider the things of old. Behold, I will do a new thing; now it shall spring forth; shall ye not know it? I will even make a way in the wilderness, and rivers in the desert. The beast of the field shall honor me, the dragons and the owls: because I give waters in the wilderness and rivers in the desert to give to my people, my chosen." The new thing God wants to do is to relocate you to the new location; to a new place in Him.

Perhaps, many of you desire to move physically speaking, to a more updated house or to a better neighborhood. You should also desire a spiritual move. You should desire to move to a deeper and wider place in God. God is going to move you to another spiritual location in Him if you will allow Him to do so. He is going to take you to another dimension in prayer, in the word, in your relationship with Him and in your destiny. You cannot excel in the assignment and purpose you were created for unless you are in the right spiritual location. The set-up is a change of mind.

God desires to change your mind about the location you are currently in. The location is new; it is fresh; it is a road in the wilderness. Yes, He wants to place a road in the mist of the desert place you are currently in, so that you will be able to travel to a new place in Him. Let Him relocate you. Let him "Position You to Live." New direction, new vision, new connections, a new attitude, new thoughts, new revelation and new insight come with a spiritual relocation. God causes rivers to flow in the desert to take you from where you are, to a new place. Rivers are a means of transportation. Rivers represent the Holy Spirit. God will, by way of the Holy Spirit, move you to your next destination in Him.

There are different spiritual locations with different levels of the anointing. Think about this: There is someone you know who has not made a spiritual move in many years. They have not repositioned themselves. Their prayer life is the same; their time studying the word is the same; their offering is the same; their sacrifices are the same. They even sit in the same place at every church service. Is this you? If so, it is time to relocate; start packing. It is time to move. God has changed your address. Know that you have got to make preparations for your move.

When you move from one house to another, planning and preparation is required. In addition, you must be willing to leave some things behind. Everything in your house cannot go to your new house. These same principles apply spiritually. You must make preparations. You must be willing to leave some things behind; including people. You have got to rid yourself of the things that are burdens; extra weight. When you move from a neighborhood that does not have ordinances to one that does, your old ways, habits and patterns of living cannot move in to the new location.

(1Kings 19:15-21) says, "And the LORD said unto him, Go, return on thy way to the wilderness of Damascus: and when thou comest, anoint Hazael to be king over Syria: And Jehu the son of Nimshi shalt thou anoint to be king over Israel: and Elisha the son of Shaphat of Abelmeholah shalt thou anoint to be prophet in thy room. And it shall come to pass, that him that escapeth the sword of Hazael shall Jehu slay: and him that escapeth from the sword of Jehu shall Elisha slay. Yet I have left me seven thousand in Israel, all the knees which have not bowed unto Baal, and every mouth which hath not kissed him. So he departed thence, and found Elisha the son of Shaphat, who was plowing with twelve yoke of oxen before him, and he with the twelfth: and Elijah passed by him, and cast his mantle upon him. And he left the oxen, and ran after Elijah, and said, Let me, I pray thee, kiss my father and my mother, and then I will follow thee. And he said unto him, Go back again: for what have I done to thee? And he returned back from him, and took a yoke of oxen, and slew them, and boiled their flesh with the instruments of the oxen, and gave unto the people, and they did eat. Then he arose, and went after Elijah, and ministered unto him."

The anointing is transferable. When you leave this earth, the anointing is transferred to your successor; to the person who continues the assignment and carries it to the next spiritual location. Elijah departs; He relocates and finds Elisha. Notice, there were eleven other teams ahead of Elisha. Just because you are last or on the back side of the desert, does not mean you are not the heir/successor. Being out front or in the back does not hinder the transfer. A few years ago, my friend needed a loan. She was hundreds of miles away in another city. We both had accounts with the same banking institution. I transferred money from my account to hers. The money was available as soon as I entered her account number and pressed send. Again, the anointing is transferable. All you need is the same Father, the same Son and the same Holy Spirit as your predecessor.

Elisha realized his set time had arrived. His set time for spiritual and natural relocation had arrived and he seized the opportunity to move; to follow God. He sensed that God was calling him to a new thing. God was calling him to move from the field to Jordan. This new line of work was Elisha's set-up. It was Elisha's time of training; a time for spiritual growth and maturity. After being under Elijah's mentorship and leadership for ten years, Elisha experienced a sequence of spiritual relocations before receiving a double portion anointing.

"And it came to pass, when the LORD would take up Elijah into heaven by a whirlwind that Elijah went with Elisha from Gilgal. And Elijah said unto Elisha, Tarry here, I pray thee; for the LORD hath sent me to Bethel. And Elisha said unto him, As the LORD liveth, and as thy soul liveth, I will not leave thee. So they went down to Bethel. And the sons of the prophets that were at Bethel came forth to Elisha, and said unto him, Knowest thou that the LORD will take away thy master from thy head to day? And he said, Yea, I know it; hold ye your peace. And Elijah said unto him, Elisha, tarry here, I pray thee; for the LORD hath sent me to Jericho. And he said, As the LORD liveth, and as thy soul liveth, I will not leave thee. So they came to Jericho. And the sons of the prophets that were at Jericho came to Elisha, and said unto him, Knowest thou that the LORD will take away thy master from thy head to day? And he answered, Yea, I know it; hold ye your peace. And Elijah said unto him, Tarry, I pray thee, here; for the LORD hath sent me to Jordan. And he said, As the LORD liveth, and as thy soul liveth, I will not leave thee. And they two went on."

Even others around him (the prophets) knew that it was the time for Elisha to relocate spiritually. They sensed that it was not God's will for Elijah to relocate spiritually and his mentee, Elisha remain in the same spiritual state. Your leader should go to higher heights and deeper depths in the anointing and so should you. I am sensing that it is time for you to be placed in the right position so that you can live. It is time for you to move from Gilgal to Bethel to Jericho and cross over into Jordan. These are the places you must travel through in the spirit to reach the greater depths of the anointing; to reach the signs, miracles and wonders anointing; to flow in the supernatural; to live the more abundant life. From this day forward remember this revelation: a servant is trained to see and sense but a successor is born to see and sense.

CHAPTER SEVEN
THE LORD HATH SENT ME

GILGAL– to roll; separation

Everyone has to go through Gilgal to reach the Jordan; the most prosperous place on the other side. Gilgal is the first spiritual location you travel through in order to live in the Glory. After leaving Egypt, which represents the world, your faith journey begins. Elisha left his father and mother's house after Elijah wrapped his cloak around him. Elisha knew in his spirit that this was the set time. This was the sign that he had been waiting on to indicate to him that it was time to move. The cloak placed the burden for ministry upon him and Elisha responded immediately. Will You Tarry in Gilgal or Will You Relocate? Could this book be your sign? Are you *Positioned to Live*?

(Joshua 4:19-20) tells us, "And the people came up out of Jordan on the tenth day of the first month, and encamped in Gilgal, in the east border of Jericho."

"And those twelve stones, which they took out of Jordan, did Joshua pitch in Gilgal. At that time the LORD said unto Joshua, Make thee sharp knives, and circumcise again the children of Israel the second time. And Joshua made him sharp knives, and circumcised the children of Israel at the hill of the foreskins. And this is the cause why Joshua did circumcise: All the people that came out of Egypt, that were males, even all the men of war, died in the wilderness by the way, after they came out of Egypt. Now all the people that came out were circumcised: but all the people that were born in the wilderness by the way as they came forth out of Egypt, them they had not circumcised. For the children of Israel walked forty years in the wilderness, till all the people that were men of war, which came out of Egypt, were consumed, because they obeyed not the voice of the LORD: unto whom the LORD sware that he would not shew them the land, which the LORD sware unto their fathers that he would give us, a land that floweth with milk and honey. And their children, whom he raised up in their stead, them Joshua circumcised: for they were uncircumcised, because they had not circumcised them by the way. And it came to pass, when they had done circumcising all the people that they abode in their places in the camp, till they were whole. And the LORD said unto Joshua, This day have I rolled away the reproach of Egypt from off you. Wherefore the name of the place is called Gilgal unto this day. And the children of Israel encamped in Gilgal, and kept the Passover on the fourteenth day of the month at evening in the plains of Jericho. And they did eat of the old corn of the land on the morrow after the Passover, unleavened cakes, and parched corn in the selfsame day. And the manna ceased on the morrow after they had eaten of the old corn of the land; neither had the children of Israel manna any more, but they did eat of the fruit of the land of Canaan that year. And it came to pass, when Joshua was by Jericho, that he lifted up his eyes and looked, and, behold, there stood a man over against him with his sword drawn in his hand: and Joshua went unto him, and said unto him, Art thou for us, or for our adversaries? And he said, Nay; but as captain of the host of the LORD am I now come. And Joshua fell on his face to the earth, and did worship, and said unto him, What saith my Lord unto his servant? And the captain of the LORD's host said unto Joshua, Loose thy shoe from off thy foot; for the place whereon thou standest is holy. And Joshua did so" (Joshua 5:2-15).

Gilgal is a place of circumcision. It is a place of cutting away and separation. It is a place where God begins to cut people out of your life. He separates you from the different systems you have grown accustom to. Those systems are a representative of mindsets; strongholds. The world system and its views; the system of self with habits; the parental system with generational traditions and curses passed down; the educational system of training to think and rationalize; the governmental system of laws, rules and regulations; the economic system of managing substance; the corporate system of analytical thinking and decision making and the entertainment system are all mindsets which have shaped you. Gilgal is a place of rolling away.

When the foreskin on a male child is circumcised, it is rolled back and cut. God rolls people out of your life and He rolls your flesh away. He rolls those cravings for the world's ways, the mindset of the world, and burdens placed on you from the world system away, and cut them off of you. Elisha was being circumcised in Gilgal. God cut away some things because he could not take Elijah's place until God cut the excess fat off of him. The unnecessary skin had to be removed. You cannot walk in the double portion anointing without a circumcision –a cutting away of flesh. Elisha could not circumcise himself. It took someone skilled in the area of ministry he was called to, to perform the incision with skillful hands. It took God working through the hands of Elijah and Joshua.

The children of Israel could not circumcise themselves. It took their leader Joshua using the right instrument to cut away the unnecessary flesh, so that God could take away the reproach of their ancestors past from the new generation. Therefore, Gilgal is a place of removing the reproach – the shame. God takes away the shame that is a result of the things you did when you were in Egypt; the world. He takes away the guilt and removes the condemnation. There is no more blaming yourself for past mistakes in Gilgal.

Gilgal is also a place of healing. After the circumcision, you begin to rest in the Lord and allow him to minister to every hurt you have sustained from the cut (lies, gossip, rejection, criticism, naysayers, backbiting, jealousy, loneliness, etc.). He begins to soothe the pain of cutting those you thought were friends, cutting the doctrine you thought was truth, cutting the soul ties you developed along the journey, cutting everything that you cannot take to Bethel. Joshua was instructed by God, to remain in Gilgal; until the people were whole. God knew that the children of Israel would not have been able to overcome their enemies in Canaan if they were still raw and bleeding from the cut.

He knows that unless you heal you want be able to: understand clearly the strategy and tactics of Satan and minister effectively to others still in Egypt. Hurting people hurt people. Even while in Gilgal the children of Israel remembered the Passover. They remembered the blood applied over their doors had caused the death angel to pass over their families. They partook in communion in Gilgal; therefore Gilgal is a place of remembering and communion. You are reminded of where God has brought you from and out of. God brings you out to bring you into a "Position to Live." When He brings you to Gilgal you cannot forget He brought you out of Egypt. If you do not humble yourself during the time of remembering, you will look down on others who are still in Egypt.

As you enter into Gilgal you will notice that your appetite changes. Here your craving for meat begins. You do not want the "ain't he alright sermon", instead, you desire revelation knowledge.

You want to know how to remain delivered. In this place, you begin to live by the word of God. You no longer live by bread alone; manna ceases. You no longer live by your flesh or your feelings. You live by every word that proceeds out of the mouth of God. And because you live by the word and the word is powerful and sharper than any two edged sword, you live by the anointing. Gilgal is a place of serving. Elisha served Elijah for ten years. It is a place of the first anointing. Elijah anointed Elisha with his cloak in Gilgal and the Prophet Samuel anointed Saul as King in Gilgal. It is a place of accepting the call. It is a place of preparation – basic training. It was the base of the children of Israel's army.

It was where they received the strategic plans on how to fight the enemy before they went out to fight. Finally, Gilgal is a place where your character is judged. The Prophet Samuel had a court in Gilgal in which he judged the people. King Saul was stripped of the kingdom in Gilgal because he performed the duties of a priest; wrong position and wrong assignment. Having the wrong character can cause you to die in your position of authority. When Jesus is being formed in you, the fruit that is produced is inspected by the Holy Spirit. Hence, this place of preparation is one that everyone must journey through in order to relocate to Bethel. Will You Tarry in Gilgal or Will You Relocate? Bethel is waiting on you.

BETHEL – the house of God

"Now the Lord had said to Abram get out of your country, from your family and from your father's house, to a land that I will show you. I will make you a great nation; I will bless you. And make your name great; And you shall be a blessing. I will bless those who bless you, And I will curse him who curses you; And in you all the families of the earth shall be blessed" (Genesis 12:1-3). God wants you to follow Him; follow His instructions.

He places a road in the desert to set you up. He does it to get you to the next level. Each location contains a blessing. Each location has something you need to acquire to strengthen your relationship with Him. That is why it is imperative that you recognize when the Glory is moving. The Glory is never a permanent settlement. The presence of God is always moving and you have got to learn how to pack up the camp and move when it moves. God did not tell Abraham where to go. He just said pack up and move — leave your country and your people.

Why did God tell Abraham to relocate? Locate means to position oneself or something to a different place or a different location. Relocate means to move again. Therefore, Abraham had moved before. This was not going to be the first time Abraham had moved to a different place; a different location. Let us look at Genesis Chapter 11. The whole earth had one language and one speech and the families of Noah journeyed or relocated and settled in the land of Shinar. They decided to build a city with a tower whose top would reach in the heavens. The Lord came down from heaven to see the city and the tower that they were building. The families were unified in every thought and work; anything they did would succeed.

God decided to confuse their language in order to stop them from building into the heavens. They started to speak in different dialects and it brought on confusion. The families developed a language barrier and the building ceased. The city was then named Babel which means confusion. Amongst the families of Noah was his son Shem in which Abraham descended. The confusion caused the families to scatter or relocate and Shem's descendants moved. Amongst those descendants who moved were Abraham's father Terah, and Nahor, Abraham's brother and Abraham. They left from a city within Babel called Ur. Ur means light and flame. There was so much confusion in the land that it dimmed the light and covered the flame. What am I saying? I am saying that you can be in a desert place even amongst light. It can be a desert for you because you have either moved too soon or too late and others around you are flourishing because it is there appointed place in that season. Abraham's father, Terah moved the family; relocated the family to Haran.

A worse place than where they moved from. Have you ever experienced leaving a bad and settled situation? And later found out that what you compromised or turned aside was even worse. So again, Abraham had moved, relocated, repositioned himself to live once before. Is there confusion where you are and the Holy Spirit has left from the midst? God is not going to tell you to leave and not tell you or show you why you have to leave (relocate). If you have to leave a place and people, there are some things you are going to go through before you reach the next location. In order to go from the north side of your city to the south side, there are things in which you must bypass before you arrive at your destination.

Bethel is place consisting of a road in the desert pointing you in the direction you need to go. Bethel means "House Of God". It is a place of seeking God. It is a place where you desire God and his presence. It is a place of hearing the word, soaking in the anointing and being *led* by the Holy Spirit. The road is a set time for a set-up. Each spiritual location is a blessing; what you need. Each location gives you something to put on for the next place in God. Abraham was 75 years old when he relocated from Haran.

Haran means parched, extremely thirsty and dry. In Haran, Abraham's relationship with God was lacking covenant; no Holy Spirit, no visions, no dreams, no intimacy. Abraham was hungry and he was thirsty for more. Abraham had to leave Haran so that God could appear to him. While in Haran, God spoke to

Abraham. It was not until he left the parched place that God appeared. God told Abraham to leave his country, his relatives and his father's house. What did God tell Abraham to forsake? God was saying Abraham I need you to let go of your government's order for heaven's order (country). I need you to let go of your traditional ways of thinking (relatives). Abraham I need you to let go of your position amongst the people and your inheritance (father's house) for your position in the Kingdom and the inheritance of heaven. You have got to get up and move and forsake some things and some people to obtain the encounter of His presence. If you are ready to transition from hearing His voice to seeing His face; you have got to relocate.

You have got to position yourself. I remember growing up in the country without cable television. We could only pick up the local channels and we had rabbit ears antennas on our television. There was also an antenna on the outside of the house that consisted of this metal tall pole. Often, someone would have to go outside and turn the pole because the reception was awful. You could not see the program but you could hear it. And that person would have to turn the outside antenna until the person on the inside of the house shouted, "The picture is showing." They had to reposition the reception. Abraham repositioned his reception and exceeded hearing the voice of God, but picked up a clear picture — the face of God. Abraham took his wife, his slaves, his cattle and his nephew Lot and he moved to the mountains that were East of Bethel.

Abraham had passed through Canaan and God showed him what He was going to give his descendents. While passing through, God even allowed Abraham to live, in the center of Canaan, in a place called Shechem. Many of you have not reached your final destination of settlement. God just intended for you to pass through; instead you have settled. Abraham lived in Canaan and so did his enemies. God does not intend for you to dwell with your enemies on a long term basis. He just wants you to remain there until He prepares a table before you in their presence. Guess what? The table goes with you when you move.

Abraham set out on a journey to acquire more than what he was getting in the desert, in the midst of the desert. Although he followed the road which led him to Bethel, he struggled with his former position in Gilgal. Abraham struggled with separating. It was a stronghold that he could not cast down; leaving Lot behind. On the road to Bethel, you will discover that there is something or some things that you will grieve to leave behind. You will struggle with the thought of letting go. You will hope that when you arrive at Bethel to worship, the Lord will not say, "They cannot remain with you." Yes, Bethel is the center of worship. It is a place where you abide under the Lord's divine protection and divine provision. It is a place of trust. It is a place of deliverance from the trap set by the enemy. It is a place where God answers and gives long life and shows His salvation.

Bethel is the House of God. The Lord said his house shall be called the house of prayer. This means that God wants to take us out of the parched place to the place of prayer. Abraham responded to God's appearance by building an altar – a place of prayer to the Lord, and he called on the name of the Lord and worshipped him.

Bethel is also a place of vision. In Bethel, the vison becomes clear with great resolution; to carry out your assignment. You begin to rest in your identification, which was revealed to you in Gilgal. You rest in who you have been called to be and what you have been called to do. In this place, you no longer worry about what people think about you. However, you have to be on alert for the spirits of arrogance, vanity and idolatry. The spirit of

53

idolatry attacks the most in this spiritual location, because you will begin to recognize the anointing on your life; others will too. They will begin to praise you and your flesh will begin to crave the praise; you must stay in the presence of the Lord.

Your gifts begin to stir up because Bethel had four springs that supplied good water. There were four rivers that flowed into Bethel which made it a watering place. It is a spiritual location to refresh, revive and restore you from the parched place you left. It is a place that strengthens your bones and causes you to be like a well-watered garden and a spring of water whose waters do not fail. Bethel is also a place of strife if you do not separate from the family member God says leave behind. Strife rose up between Abraham and Lot in Bethel because Abraham could not cut the umbilical cord when the Lord said leave your family in Haran – the parched place. Abraham had taken Lot to Bethel; to Egypt and back to Bethel. God allowed the strife in order for His perfect will to be manifested. In the midst of the strife, Abraham decreed the original plan of God. He told Lot, "Please separate from me". You have to position yourself to live like Abraham.

If Abraham had continued to share his destiny with Lot, he would have forfeited his inheritance. He would have deprived his grandson Jacob of an encounter with the Lord. In Genesis 28, Jacob relocates from Beersheba. On the run from the consequences of his lies, Jacob goes toward Haran and came to a certain place. This place was his set-up for a visitation from the Lord. The sun goes down. Jacob camps there for the night; not knowing this was a place of dreams, visions and rest. Jacob has a vision of angels descending and ascending from heaven to the earth. This reveals that Bethel is a place of an open heaven, deliverance and resting in identity. A place where you give thanks unto the Lord and He sends angels with your deliverance and gives your heart desires.

54

Lord appears and makes known to Jacob that He is the Lord of his grandfather Abraham and his father Isaac. God reaffirms His promise to give the inheritance to the descendants of Abraham. Abraham's destiny could not support himself and Lot. Your destiny cannot, will not, does not support you and those who God has said release from your life. Why did God say release them? He's trying to get you in the "Position to Live."

JERICHO– walk by faith

Jericho was in the plain of Jordan, over against the place where the river was crossed by the Israelites. It was the most important city in the Jordan valley and the strongest fortress in all the land of Canaan. It was the "holy land"– the first blessing; the beginning of the Abrahamic promise. It was the first city that the children of Israel possessed. It was the best portion of all the land promised by God. In Exodus 34, God showed Moses all the land promised to his people. Moses could not see the land from the valley. He had to go to the top of the mountain and the Lord caused him to see all of the promise land. Moses died. He did not enter into the land because of his double sin of not believing God and not hallowing Him. The Lord allowed the children of Israel to mourn for him 30 days. Then the Lord said to Joshua, "Moses My servant is dead. Now therefore, arise, go over this Jordan, you and all this people, to the land which I am giving to them – the children of Israel" (Joshua 1:2).

Before you move into the spiritual location of Jericho, something has to die. That something could be that marriage that is not working out or that friend who turned their back or that business deal that went south. Everyone has a Moses. And if you want to cross over into the promise God has promised you, you have got to get up from where you are and move! It is time to move! Go forward! You must get ***Positioned to Live***.

When I was in basic training in Fort Dix, New Jersey, I had to complete a 15 mile road march. I was fully equipment in military gear; carrying an M-16. Throughout the entire basic training each soldier had a "buddy". Your "buddy" was the soldier your Drill Sergeant paired you up with; a brother's keeper. You had to know where your "buddy" was and what your "buddy" was doing at all times. If your "buddy" was in trouble, you were in trouble. If your "buddy" got behind during the march, you were responsible for helping your "buddy" to catch up. You were responsible for positioning your "buddy" to live. I was the guide arm bearer. This is the soldier in front of the platoon carrying the flag – identifying who you are. When my "buddy" got behind, I had to leave my position out front and go get my "buddy" and place her back in her appointed position in the platoon. Then I had to go back to my position and continue to lead the platoon. Regardless of how many times my "buddy" got behind, I had to have the endurance. I had more weight to carry than the rest of the soldiers. I had to carry the identity – the flag. I had to run with the identity – the flag, get my "buddy" and help her get back in her appointed position and run back to my appointed position and lead.

This is what Jericho represents: enduring the tests of your identity. Joshua had been placed in a position to live not for himself but for the people. Jericho is a place where the position is not about you; it is about the family's deliverance. You have been trained in Bethel to tap into the spirit in your time of prayer and worship and to download heaven's instructions. In this place, the enemy attacks your seed the most and you have got to be prepared to fight before you enter into the gate of the city.

Before you go into the enemy's camp and take back what he has stolen from you, you have another preparation period.

Joshua went throughout the camp commanding the children of Israel to "prepare provisions" for three days. You have got to prepare your spirit for that which awaits you in Jericho. You have got to feast on the word day and night. You cannot live by bread alone. You must live by every word that proceeds out of the mouth of the Lord. Jericho is a place of standing on the word of God.

The proceeding word is instructions on how to defeat those who are living in your land. Jericho is a place where the wicked are judged before the eyes of the righteous. There are many enemies in Jericho and they are idol worshippers. They even sacrificed their children. Therefore, this is the place where the anointing on your life exposes idolatry and the occult (witchcraft). Not only do you exposed them, but God trains and instructed you on how to destroy them. God allowed the children of Israel to kill all the men, women, children and cattle of their enemies. All spoils of the city were destroyed. In this place, you let go of everything that is going to spoil your assignment. This includes breaking ties with people that are going to destroy the assignment that is on your life. You do not have time to decide on whether or not you should break the ties. God said, "Do it." And God said, "keep the silver, gold, bronze and iron and spare the prostitute – Rahab, her father's house and all she has." Jericho is a place where you move from praying for deliverance to becoming the deliverer. You carry an anointing to shift the atmosphere in the person's life when you cross the gate of Jericho. This is the sign that God gives when your ministry has changed and shifted.

Those you are assigned to deliver are drawn to your fragrance in the spirit. The Arabic meaning of Jericho is fragrance/scent. The scent of the glory that is on your life attracts them to the deliverance within you. No matter how they try to fight against the scent, the deliverance anointing overpowers their fight. God wants to position them to live. He wants to use you to set the captive free so they can move into their divine position, their divine assignment and their divine destiny. And he reveals their position, assignment and destiny to you in intercession. Jericho is the place where you are interceding on the behalf of the people. The burden for the people is like a consuming fire. It overtakes you and positions you in a place in the spirit to birth their deliverance. In order to do this, you have got to be led by the Holy Spirit.

In Jericho, the Lord teaches you how to tame your tongue; how to use the weapon of silence. He instructs you on what to say and when to say it. He also teaches you how to wait in silence. The children of Israel were instructed to march around the wall of Jericho one time for six days in silence and wait on God to move. The priests were out front blowing the trumpets; followed by the Ark of the Covenant and the children of Israel. The Ark of the Covenant represented the presence of God; the Glory of God. The Glory is what leads you into Jericho. You have to be led by the Glory and be a carrier of the Glory. You have to be conditioned to carry the weight of the Glory.

This spiritual location requires consecration, purification, sanctification, denying of self and carrying your cross. Carrying your cross conditions you to carry the weight of His Glory. On the seventh day the Lord said this time you can say something – shout. Joshua told the children of Israel to shout for the Lord has given you the city. As you begin to walk in the anointing of a tamed tongue, when it is time to speak, it is also time to see the results of what was spoken. Every wall must come down. Every stronghold and every imagination that exalts itself above the knowledge of Jesus Christ has to fall and bow.

Now arise. Get up from where you are and go to the next dimension. Go to the next dimension in prayer. Go to the next height in worship. Go to the next depth in your relationship with God. Go to the next level in your dreams and visions. Arise! Take up your bed and walk in the spirit. Arise out of that dead ministry. Arise out of that dead relationship. Arise out of that dead business deal. Stop murmuring and complaining about it!

God is trying to take you to another place – Jericho. Arise, go and do not look back. Your more abundant life is in forward movement. Looking back puts you at risk of becoming a pillar of salt which never moves again. You have to go through Jericho in order to get to Jordan. This requires walking by faith and not by sight. Faith produces the fullness of the Abrahamic blessing – the promise. And no man can stand against you all the days of your life because you are *Positioned to Live.*

JORDAN – the watering place; descender
Your time of refreshing and restoration is here – in Jordan. The River of Jordan flows into four streams and empties all the waste it has collected over time into the Dead Sea. This represents all the filth that others tried to place on you throughout your travels; all the lies, gossip, naysaying, back-biting, incantations, slander, ridicule, false accusations, character assassination, etc. Here in Jordan you rid yourself of others opinions and thoughts about your position and your assignment. You have settled in your identity and the prophetic word(s) has settled in your heart. The spirit of the Lord is leading you into the written word as it manifests the spoken word.

This is the place of the Oasis. You are now a fertile ground in the midst of a desert place; where travelers replenish their water supplies from your reservoir. You are now in a place of administering relief from a troubling and/or chaotic situation because the reach has extended beyond your household and beyond the walls of the church. This is the spiritual location that elevates the call to the nations. It extends to the international ministry; to the masses. It requires a breaking, a making over, a rebuilding. It is a place of humility. It is a place of compassion and love for the people. To whom much is given, much is required is carved as a brand and a seal in your spirit in this place. The carving is the final separation from that that is hindering your ministry. It is a place where you are placed on the operating room table without anesthesia.

An incision is made straight down your chest and your chest cavity is stretched wide open. And Jesus goes to work and begins to form Himself in you. It is a place where the pain is excruciating beyond consciousness. It is the garden of Gethsemane's reality. Jordan is a place of crucifixion and resurrection, so that the anointing for the greater work can begin to flow out of you. The greater work is the work of the supernatural. It is the place where the double portion anointing of Elijah is conferred on the Elisha ministry; the ministry of miracles, signs and wonders. In (2 Kings 2:7), Elijah and Elisha stood by the Jordan and Elijah took his mantle, rolled it up and struck the water. It divided and they crossed over the Jordan. In (Joshua 3:17), the priest placed the sole of their feet in the Jordan, while carrying the Ark of the Covenant (the Glory), and the Jordan stopped flowing, divided and the children of Israel crossed over. In Jordan, your communion changes with God and with your spiritual father. You elevate from relationship, to fellowship, to friendship, to followship.

The elevations position you to live while carrying out your assignment on the earth. The evidence that you are in the right position, performing the right assignment is that you are bearing much fruit and it is remaining. The remaining fruit is the seed promise manifested by the Glory. Now, you are "*Positioned to Live*." You have been baptized in the Jordan and the spirit of God has descended down upon you. The voice of God has spoken from the heavens saying, "I am well pleased."